FREE AND FAITHFUL

FREE AND FAITHFUL

BAPTISTS

CHRISTIAN DISCIPLESHIP IN THE TWENTY-FIRST CENTURY

DWIGHT A. MOODY

PROVIDENCE HOUSE PUBLISHERS
Franklin, Tennessee

Printed in the United States of America

02   01   00   99   98   1   2   3   4   5

Library of Congress Catalog Card Number: 98-65355

ISBN: 1-57736-097-4

Cover design by Gary Bozeman

Scripture taken from the HOLY BIBLE, NEW INTERNATIONAL VERSION. Copyright 1973, 1978, 1984 International Bible Society. Used by permission of Zondervan Bible Publishers.

PROVIDENCE HOUSE PUBLISHERS
238 Seaboard Lane • Franklin, Tennessee 37067
800-321-5692

In Gratitude To

My Parents

Tom and Reita Moody

to whom this book is dedicated
in recognition
of the attractive way in which they embody
free and faithful Christ-centered living;

My secretary, Debbie Sanders, for the patient and professional way in which she prepared these sermon manuscripts;

My friend John Williams, whose generosity made possible the publication of this book;

Pastors Jimmy Gentry and Paul Basden, professor Roger Ward, and editor Debbie Sims for the careful reading of the text and;

My friend Brad Baker, professional orthodontist and amateur photographer, whose pictures adorn the cover of the book.

CONTENTS

PREFACE

During the summer of 1994, while serving as pastor of Third Baptist Church of Owensboro, Kentucky, I preached a series of sermons on the religious and theological traditions of Baptists. This grew out of two very important events, one social, the other personal. The first of these was the transformation of the Southern Baptist Convention. I had been nurtured from birth in the convictions and culture of this religious vision. It was a mixture of joy and guilt, learning and prejudice, salvation and damnation, and it took hold of my soul and called me to be its servant.

My pilgrimage took me to Georgetown College, one of our Baptist affiliated colleges, then to Jerusalem for a glorious year of travel and study; finally to what was then considered the principal center of Baptist learning in all the world, Southern Baptist Theological Seminary of Louisville, Kentucky. Before I could complete my academic work, the entire convention was engulfed in a struggle of self-definition. People, powerful people, had a very different sense of what it meant to be Baptist, and they succeeded in seizing the institutional means of establishing and extending their version of Baptist life and thought. Perhaps they were the family back home that I found embarrassing; perhaps they were the in-laws that married into the family bringing with them new patterns of speech and conduct. The family reunions, so to speak, became occasions overrun by strangers; some found them happy, I found them depressing.

Like many who had called themselves Baptist, I struggled to find my place in this new family of faith. The spirit and substance of the conversation was foreign to my life in Christ. I asked myself: Are these people Baptists? Am I a Baptist? Why is everything so strange, such a struggle? I was forced to evaluate the shape and substance of my own identity as a Baptist Christian. Reading, writing, talking, listening, praying, waiting, and yes, preaching— these were the elements of my search, these were the paths I walked on my journey.

There were, I discovered, many who were walking this way, indeed many who had walked this way before. Among these was James William McClendon Jr., and the Jr. is important. He was a southerner of the Texas variety, a theologian, a thinker, a teacher, a writer. I read first his book *Ethics*, then the wonderful *Doctrine*; and therein I found a vision of Baptist ways that was both fresh and familiar. He was describing the kind of Christian I had always been; he was explaining the things I had always believed. And the ironic beauty of it all was his testimony to a similar, self-clarifying experience at the same midpoint of his intellectual and spiritual life, on which occasion he picked up the writings of John Howard Yoder and discovered himself.

McClendon is now my friend, and his books fill a shelf in my library. Most of all, his ideas and his manner of expression have given new enthusiasm to the confession and conduct of my own faith. As a tribute to his influence and as a statement of my refurbished life as a Baptist, I have adopted here and elsewhere McClendon's peculiar use of the word *baptist*. By this word, he (and I) refer to a way of being Christian, a pattern of following Christ, a vision of Christian existence—initiated by Anabaptist ancestors in the 1500s. Sometimes, this *way*, this pattern, this vision finds visible expression in organizations, institutions, and agencies known by the name Baptist. At other times, Baptists drift from the baptist vision; this has happened, so I judge, among some known as Southern Baptists.

These intellectual and spiritual forces, pushing and pulling, formed the context of both my personal and my pastoral work. For I was also very much concerned with the mental fuzziness of my own congregation concerning the chief ideas and practices of the baptist Christian tradition. Our church, like all churches, needed constant exposure to, and examination of, the essential themes of our faith.

Much has been written about the current decline in denominational awareness and loyalty. The response to the corresponding rise in generic Christianity is mixed. Some press more firmly the importance of a particular religious network (like the Southern Baptist Convention) while others abandon all heritages and opt for the paradigm of disconnected church life. I have traveled another road, one pioneered by McClendon and others, a road that leads to this affirmation: God called out baptist people in order to bless and serve the entire Christian community.

Out of my own religious struggles and out of the need of my congregation these sermons came. Their purpose is to give faithful, explicit instruction in how the baptist interpretation of Scripture gives rise to the life and work of baptists. This, in turn, equips baptists for our role in the Christian mission of the twenty-first century. May we all be faithful to the calling which we have received from our wise and gracious God.

For the glory of God and the common good
Georgetown College, February, 1998

FREE AND FAITHFUL DISCIPLES

He answered, "I have lost all interest in baptist things." So spoke a prominent theologian who had been a Southern Baptist. I had expressed interest in a particular aspect of baptist theology. "I am more interested," he continued, "in the broader issues of evangelical theology. I think that is the real need of today." He is not alone in his conviction. A similar stance was taken by a man who recently served as president of the Southern Baptist Convention. Soon after his election, he said, "I could very easily be a Presbyterian."

There is a certain legitimacy to the thinking of these two men. They sense the need to de-emphasize those things that are distinctly baptist and give priority to those things that we share in common with other Christians and with other evangelicals. I recently noted an advertisement in a Baptist periodical calling for applications and recommendations for faculty positions at the Southern Baptist Theological Seminary. After stating academic credentials, the notice stated applicants must adhere to a theological position that is "conservative evangelical." There was no reference to "Baptists."

The writing of baptist theologians gives evidence of the same perspective. During the last fifteen years, there has been a host of systematic theology books written by persons affiliated with the baptist tradition. It is quite interesting that most of these give little attention to the baptist tradition, opting instead for standard and rather predictable presentations of what can also be called "conservative evangelical" theology. This demonstrates the powerful tendency for baptist theologians to de-emphasize those things that are distinctive of the baptist tradition.

This book is a protest against this situation, at both the congregational and the theological level. I am not so sure this abdication of baptist principles is in the best interest of baptist church life or that it offers a better strategy for addressing the myriad challenges to Christian faith and living today. I wish to make a case that our best contribution to the Christian movement is by being baptist.

It is no progress to reduce all Christian living, believing and confessing to some generic brand of religion. Rather, we enrich the Christian church when we articulate our faith as we see it through the prism of baptist life. We follow God's purpose for us when we live our faith as we understand it through the traditions of baptists. Do we not believe that God in keeping with His sovereign will has raised up the people called baptists for a specific purpose? Can not this purpose be stated as two-fold? For the glory of God and the good of the world. In other words, does not God wish to bless the entire Christian community through the unique insights, traditions and convictions of baptists?

The church of Jesus Christ is like an orchestra. Each church and denomination plays its part. Catholics exemplify order, continuity and loyalty. Presbyterians teach us about the sovereignty of God and the centrality of Scripture. Methodists brought to us new emphasis on revivals and spiritual disciplines. Pentecostals reintroduced healing to the modern church and embody what it means for the church to be a counter-culture to the prevailing secularism of our day.

Baptists can learn from others. While in Jerusalem in May of 1994, we worshiped at the Lutheran Church of the Redeemer in the Old City. I was impressed chiefly by one thing. Through three readings of Scripture, several prayers, and the recitation of a confession of faith, the entire gospel was fully declared. Baptists would do well to learn from the Lutherans to declare our faith in more public and explicit ways. This is one of the strengths of protestant worship.

Baptists also make their contribution to this Christian symphony. We play our instrument and add our distinctive sound. What would an orchestra be if all people played the same instrument? Even when playing the same note and tune, it is the variety of instruments that give the concert its rich and compelling texture. We welcome the sound of the French horn, viola, oboe and timpani. Baptists are a small part of the great Christian orchestra, but the sound and quality of our part is of real importance.

Furthermore, music lovers delight in the presence of sub-themes and minor movements when listening to the great compositions. They add drama and suspense, depth and beauty. Such is the contribution of baptists. We are, in many ways, a dissenting people. We emphasize things (like believer's baptism by immersion and the separation of church and state) that are not embraced by the majority of Christians. We play our minor melodies confident that, in God's providence, we contribute to the beauty and power of the whole.

I affirm our baptist identify, not because we are perfect, or because we have all the answers, or even because we are designated to carry the major theme. Rather, we have our convictions, our heritage, our understanding of the gospel which we believe is from God. Can we not believe that God will bless all of His people, and indeed, the entire world because of the way baptist people believe and behave the gospel?

This way of understanding the baptist vision frees us from a narrow, sectarian pride than rejects all who differ as heretics, as living in disobedience to the Lord Jesus Christ. The Apostle Paul likened the Church to a body with many parts.

> The body is a unit, though it is made up of many parts; and though all its parts are many, they form one body. So it is with Christ. . . . Now you are the body of Christ, and each one of you is a part of it. (1 Cor. 12:12, 27)

This insight applies not only to individuals who have different gifts, but also to congregations and traditions.

No one Christian group can affirm, embody and implement all of the wide and wonderful truth of God's Word. Each lives out the gospel in accordance with its God-given vision of Christian existence. This is not to say there is no error or misconstrual of God's ways and words—surely, baptists, catholics, and protestants alike fall short of perfection in things theological, ethical and spiritual. The preface to "The Confession of Faith of those Churches which are commonly (though falsely) called Anabaptist," now known as the London Confession of 1644, expresses this awareness of possible error and ignorance when it confesses that "we believe the Lord will daily cause truth more to appear in the hearts of his saints."

With this attitude toward the proper place of the baptist vision in the life of the Christian church, we can sound clearly the dual notes of baptist life and work, freedom and faithfulness. A good Scripture summary of these things is found in Galatians chapter five, verses one and thirteen:

> It is for freedom that Christ has set us free. Stand firm, then, and do not let yourselves be burdened again by a yoke of slavery. . . .
> You, my people, were called to be free. But do not use your freedom to indulge the sinful nature; rather, serve one another in love.

What are the focal points of these verses? Freedom and faithfulness. These are precisely the two foci of baptist theology and spirituality. We can consider first freedom and then faithfulness.

BAPTIST MEANS FREEDOM

Baptist love of freedom at both the personal and corporate level is set over against the catholic vision of order. During the summer of 1994, the Roman Catholic pope issued his encyclical entitled, "On Reserving Priestly Ordination to Men Alone." The baptist way presents a sharp dissent from three elements of this papal decree. First, this encyclical is one person making decisions for other people. Second, it sets limits on what God can do in the life of another person. Third, it calls for all further discussion and dissension to cease. It is hard to imagine an illustration more firmly turned against the baptist understanding of freedom in the things of the spirit.

Against this sort of authoritarian understanding of spiritual things, baptists sound their note of freedom. Baptists are free before God, with no priest or preacher, pastor or pope to dictate to us how to come into the Lord's presence or what to say in His name. Baptists are free in the Word of God, unbounded by creeds, confessions of faith or decisions of any council of men or women. Baptists are free in the church, with each person energized by the gift-giving Spirit. Baptists are free in the world, organizing and mobilizing for ministry and evangelism without the constraints of secular and ecclesiastical power.

BAPTIST MEANS FAITHFULNESS

But freedom is not all there is to being a baptist kind of Christian. Baptist means faithfulness. Thus our text declares in no uncertain terms: "Do not use your freedom to indulge the sinful nature." Freedom without direction and discipline is chaos. The hymn "America The Beautiful" implores God to "confirm thy soul in self-control, thy liberty in law."

A little history helps us understand the baptist way of faithfulness. The baptist movement arose from the medieval confusion called Christendom. Throughout Christianized Europe, babies were baptized and considered church members without regard to their actual living or confessing as followers of Christ. It was the pattern of nominal Christianity, that is, Christian in name only. Against this distortion of biblical religion, baptists contended for a certain kind of faithfulness in Christian discipleship. We insisted on a personal, intelligent, voluntary commitment to the life and teaching of Jesus prior to the public rite of initiation, baptism.

This, of course, did not assure that all baptized people would continue in their Christian pilgrimage, but it did clarify the priority which baptists placed on intentional discipleship.

In our day, nominal Christianity is again a major problem. There are many churches like Third Baptist Church of Owensboro, where I served as pastor, with hundreds of members who never attend worship, rarely open the Bible, and ignore basic responsibility to witness and support missions and ministries around the world. It is church membership without participation, profession without practice, baptism without discipleship, lip service without life service. Like Christian identity bestowed by infant baptism, this pattern of church life contradicts the baptist insight into the nature of salvation.

Baptist means faithfulness. It is faithfulness to the call of God in Jesus through a life of discipleship. It is faithfulness to the Word of God—reading, learning, believing, obeying, hiding it in our heart that we might not sin against God. It is faithfulness to the church through a covenant relationship. It is faithfulness to the world, ministering and evangelizing in the name of Jesus Christ.

It is the purpose and intent of God for baptist people, free and faithful, to sound out these notes. We do our part in the life and work of the worldwide church of Jesus Christ when we bear witness to the way Jesus Christ is known and experienced in and through a church of baptist people. Not everybody is called to be a baptist; but baptists are called to be baptists. By being faithful to our calling we help the church of Jesus Christ reach her full potential in the power and wisdom of the Holy Spirit.

So I conclude that it is a mistake for baptist people to jettison baptist ideals and convictions, to tone down our own unique heritage in Christ, in an effort to merge all Christians toward some common, generic version of Christian faith. Some who have abandoned the baptist vision seem proud that they have relieved themselves of the idiosyncrasies of some peculiar, even embarrassing minority, in an effort to embrace what they consider the broad, clear principles of the Christian mainstream. But I dissent.

Perhaps a word picture from the famous Oxford don C. S. Lewis will help bring balance to this tension between the generic and the particular. Lewis is the Anglican scholar who popularized the concept of "mere Christianity." In the preface to *Mere Christianity*, he likens the Church to a great cathedral. It has a central hall into which people come. For Lewis, this represents the common elements of the Christian religion. It is "mere Christianity"—what I earlier called "generic religion." Lewis felt it was his calling to help people enter this great hall. But he also said that connected to this great hall are side rooms. It is here that people eat and sleep, speak and are spoken to. In these side rooms we find nourishment and friendship and partnership in the things of God. Do not stay long in the great hall, he urged. Find one of the side rooms and enter into the fellowship of Christian people.

One of those side rooms is the baptist hall. There, baptist folk worship, minister, think, and confess like baptist people. It is a good room, a healthy room, a friendly room open to new people. I invite you to enter the great hall of Jesus. But I also invite you to enter the warm, friendly, gracious room of baptists. It will do you good, if you enter under the leading of the spirit of God. And it will do good to the entire household of faith if we maintain the life and work that has been a feature of this room for more than four centuries.

CHAPTER ONE

FREE BEFORE GOD

NAME YOUR DAUGHTERS HANNAH

Baptist parents would do well to name their daughters Hannah. Her story is told in 1 Samuel. It illustrates the most basic principle of baptist-style religion: freedom before God. Hannah was one of two wives of Elkanah. She had no children, and this was a burden to her. Elkanah and Hannah lived in Ramathaim, in the hill country north of Jerusalem. They worshiped at Shiloh. The biblical narrative recounts how Hannah

> In bitterness of soul, wept much and prayed to the Lord . . . "O Lord Almighty, if you will only look upon your servant's misery and remember me . . . but give her a son, then I will give him to the Lord for all the days of his life. . . ." (1 Sam. 1:10-11)

The priest Eli was observing this scene "sitting on a chair by the door post." He thought Hannah was drunk, because while she prayed, her lips moved but she did not speak. In other words, she was praying to the Lord silently. She prayed an extemporaneous prayer, without the aid or assistance of priest or prayer book. Eli interrupted her praying with a sharp rebuke, "Hannah, get rid of your wine!" But Hannah replied, "I am pouring out my soul to the Lord." Eli then bestowed a blessing upon Hannah with these words, "Go in peace and may the God of Israel grant you what you have asked of him" (1 Sam. 1:12-17).

Hannah was engaged in the most basic act of the Christian believer, talking directly with God. Hannah was free before God. She was unhindered by the need for any human assistance—no written material, no religious professional, no monetary fee, no traditional ritual. Hannah was one soul, created in God's image, in need of what only the Lord could provide. She came directly to God.

This is the way Jesus prayed. He talked to God about the needs of his life. He received direction from God. He taught us to pray this way. Go into a closet, he said, and there present your needs to your heavenly Father. Ask of God, and you will receive.

The unnamed apostolic author of Hebrews describes our freedom with these words

> Therefore, since we have a great high priest, . . . Jesus the Son of God . . . let us then approach the throne of grace with confidence, so that we may receive mercy and find grace to help us in our time of need. (Heb. 4:14–16)

E. Y. Mullins, the great Baptist leader of the first part of the twentieth century, writes of this truth in his famous book *The Axioms of Religion*. He states the religious axiom with these words, "All people have an equal right to direct access to God." In the revised edition of that little book prepared by Herschel H. Hobbs and published by Broadman Press, these words of explanation are given:

> This axiom simply asserts the inalienable right of every person to deal with God for himself. . . . It is based upon the principle of the soul's competency in religion. It asserts that on the question of spiritual privilege there are no such differences in human nature as warrant our drawing a line between people and claiming for one group in this particular what cannot be claimed for others. It denies that there are any obstacles to any believing soul to any part of the Father's grace. There can, therefore, be no special classes in religion. All have equal access to the Father's table, the Father's ear, and the Father's heart.

Sometimes this part of the baptist vision is termed "soul competency." At other times it is called "priesthood of the believer" (although I think this is much too narrow a definition for this Reformation phrase). Smyth and Helwys Publishing of Macon, Georgia, has taken this theme of personal freedom in religion as a major focus of their publishing.

Freedom before God is, by whatever phrase it is signified, an essential element of the baptist experience of God. This precious understanding of true religion is cultivated by such practices as a preference for spontaneous prayer as opposed to prepared prayers, lay leadership and participation in worship and Bible study, discussion rather than lecture as a leadership style, family devotions and prayers, use of personal rather than pew Bibles, and the importance given to personal testimony of individual encounters with the living God.

There are likewise many ways that this freedom is denied or compromised. It is denied by traditions that encourage people to pray to God through Mary, or saints, or even religious professionals like priests and pastors. It is hindered by parents who do not provide their children the opportunity to read the Bible, worship God, and pray. It is compromised by liturgies that restrict the prayer of the people, individually or collectively, to the words written by some other person.

Freedom before God is distorted by religious leaders—Catholic, Protestant, even some who claim to be Baptist—who promote the idea that they are the ones chosen by God to hear His voice and discern His will. It is repudiated by people who refuse to take responsibility for their own spiritual life, moral discernment, and eternal destiny.

Hannah worshiped God in the spirit and style of baptist people everywhere. Her heart was burdened. She chose her own time and place to pray. She lifted up to God a prayer in her own words. Hannah was free before God.

Freedom as exercised by Hannah will not, of course, be independent of a praying community. In such company, our prayer life is shaped by the patterns and processes of other people. Prayer that is memorized, written, read, or recited often forms the rich resources out of which comes prayer that is free, spontaneous, and shaped by the burdens and blessings of the moment. As we read in private or in public the many prayers recorded in Scripture, we gain new freedom to range far and wide in giving voice to the yearnings of our hearts.

Spiritual freedom, like all freedom, brings accountability. Only the free person is responsible for his thoughts and deeds. Free baptists come before a free God accountable for our sins, responsible for hearing and heeding the voice of God. Those who are free in the presence must respond with repentance and with obedience. Section nine of the Short Confession of Faith in XX Articles by John Smyth (1609) says this well.

> That men, of the grace of God through the redemption of Christ, are able . . . to repent, to believe, to turn to God and to attain to eternal life; so on the other hand, they are able themselves to resist the Holy Spirit, to depart from God, and to perish for ever [sic].

This great truth of the free soul undergirds the preaching of all the prophets, the apostles and our Lord himself. "Repent, and believe the Good News. Follow me. Enter the kingdom."

This spiritual freedom, like all freedom, brings opportunity. Only the free person can experience all the richness of God's glory and goodness. Free baptists can know the salvation of God, the forgiveness of sin, the gift of the Holy Spirit, the sweetness of Christian fellowship. All the promises of God, for this life and the next, are available to those who freely and without hindrance, call upon the name of the Lord. What does the Scripture say? "Those who call upon the Lord will not be disappointed"(Joel 2:32, Rom. 10:13).

Eli was priest of the Most High God. But he learned something very important that day in the house of God at Shiloh. He learned anew the meaning of freedom before God. When Hannah explained what she was doing, Eli could have rebuked her for praying in that way, for not requesting his assistance, for ignoring the written prayer guides, for failure to pray at the proper time or with the proper position. Instead, he blessed her. There is a blessing for every person who lives in this wonderful world of freedom.

Like Eli, baptists and indeed Christians of all persuasions need to be reminded of the value, even the necessity, of freedom in our dealings with God. It falls to baptists to forever hold high the banner of freedom.

There are times, obviously, when the values of freedom and liberty seem to conflict with the values of order and authority. This happens in things political as well as things ecclesiastical. When these two necessary elements collide, how should baptists react? While each situation is different, it is important for baptists to realize that it is our calling before God to emphasize the freedom dimension of Christian life and thought.

Let us articulate the good gifts that come through our freedom in Christ; let others urge the necessity of order and authority. In this way, do we not take the role of Hannah in the biblical story? Does not Eli play the authoritarian part, seeking to control how and when and where Hannah could exercise her spiritual rights? Is it not Hannah who is nearer to the heart of God in this matter? Was it not God who blessed Hannah through the words of Eli?

Name your daughter Hannah. Steep her soul in the prayers and promises of both the people of God and the word of God. Then she shall be free indeed to commune with One who loves her and calls her into holy conversation.

CHAPTER TWO

FAITHFUL TO GOD

RAISED TO WALK IN NEWNESS OF LIFE

Recent books and articles on church growth often list the characteristics of the baby boomer generation. One of these is low denominational identity and loyalty. This means that young adults are less concerned with denominational labels and affiliations than they are with the actual life of a particular local congregation. They are interested in positive worship experiences, quality children's programs, and need-based teaching. This market force has pushed many congregations away from historic traditions and toward a generic brand of Christian religion. This has become one of the dominant trends in American church life.

This book is, in some sense, a response to this trend. It is a defense of the baptist way of knowing and living Jesus Christ. I contend that God raised up the people called baptists to enrich the church of Jesus Christ. God gave to the people called baptists an insight into the gospel that makes our way of living out the gospel something of value to the world.

What is that *something?* It is the way we emphasize two aspects of the biblical revelation: freedom and faithfulness. Like all other Christians, it is not what we affirm that sets us apart, but rather what we emphasize. Let me expand upon this idea. Christians (and congregations) often read the same biblical text, affirm the truth of the entire narrative or admonition, but emphasize one element that in turn shapes their vision of the Christian life.

The second chapter of Acts is the story of how the Holy Spirit comes upon the followers of Jesus and empowers them to speak in tongues and declare the gospel. Some read this text, focus on the fact that the Spirit comes to women and men, and thereby find scriptural motivation for seeking gender equality in the Church. Others read this story, highlight the gift of speaking in tongues, and hence feel compelled to seek this gift for themselves, even for all believers. Still others read the narrative and are moved by how the apostles proclaimed the good things of God so that all heard in their own language, and therefore sense a call to the missionary and evangelistic task. And finally there are those who read the chapter, seize upon the command to believe and be baptized, and therein discover the mandate to insist upon baptism as a condition for salvation.

All four readers would *affirm* the total truth and usefulness of every aspect of the text; all affirm it as the Word of God. But it is what is *emphasized* that shapes Christian living in such radically different ways.

What is true of one biblical text is true of the entire Bible. It is not so much what is affirmed about the Bible that shapes who we are and how we live as Christians, as it is what we are called to emphasize. Baptists are those people who emphasize those texts and traditions that undergird freedom and faithfulness in the things of Christ.

We believe in freedom before God, freedom in the Word, freedom in the church, and freedom in the world. Likewise, baptists are called to be faithful to God, faithful to the Word, faithful to the church, and faithful to the world. The focus of this chapter is faithfulness to God.

Paul the Apostle speaks to this issue in the sixth chapter of Romans.

> We were buried with him through baptism into death in order that, just as Christ was raised from the dead

> through the glory of the Father, we too may live a new
> life. . . . We know that our old self was crucified with him
> so that the body of sin might be done away with, that we
> should no longer be slaves to sin. . . . Therefore do not let
> sin reign in your mortal body so that you obey its evil
> desires . . . but rather offer yourselves to God as those
> who have been brought from death to life, and offer the
> parts of your body to him as instruments of righteous-
> ness. (Rom. 6:1–3)

Baptists often read this passage because it speaks of baptism.
Baptism is indeed one of the distinctive features of baptist life. For
almost ten years, I pastored a church in Pittsburgh, Pennsylvania.
Baptists in Pittsburgh are a distinct minority; for many of our
friends, we were the only baptists they knew. Therefore, believer's
baptism by immersion was unusual. Most Christians in the area
had never seen a baptist-style baptism or had never heard an intelligent rationale for such a practice. It was quite common for people
who were being baptized to invite their friends and relatives to the
service. Recently, a pastor sent to me a baptismal invitation used
by his congregation to encourage attendance of friends and relatives at a service of believer's baptism.

It is not, however, the mode of baptism that is of chief importance. Paul does not deal directly with how a person is baptized
(although the image of dying and rising is very suggestive); rather
he dwells on why a person is baptized. The *manner* is not as important as the *meaning*.

Baptism means the leaving of an old life of sin and the beginning of a new life of righteousness. Baptism signals the conversion
of the sinner. Baptism initiates the Christian life of a person who
has confessed Jesus as Lord. In other words, baptism is a ceremony
for believers.

The Schleitheim Confession, one of the early baptistic confessions of faith dating from 1525, reads like this:

> Baptism shall be given to all those who have learned
> repentance and amendment of life, and who believe truly
> that their sins are taken away by Christ, and to all those

who walk in the resurrection of Jesus Christ, and wish to
be buried with Him in death, so that they may be resur-
rected with Him, and to all those who with this
significance request it of us and demand it for themselves.
This excludes all infant baptism, the highest and chief
abomination of the pope.

The baptist movement began as a protest against the baptism of
infants and all of its consequences. Infants were (and are) baptized
as Christians without ever hearing, understanding, or confessing
the Gospel. This breeds a nominal kind of faith, one in which
neither conversion nor discipleship is emphasized. Baptists insisted
on the call to radical discipleship; those wishing to be named as
believers must live a focused and disciplined Christian life.

This raises an interesting question. Baptists contend that
believer's baptism is more effective than infant baptism in
developing mature, disciplined followers of Jesus. Is this so?
Would not a study comparing baptist churches with Protestant or
Catholic churches shed light on this matter? If believer's baptism
does result in more growth in the grace and knowledge of Christ,
would not this provide confirmation of our contention that a
disciplined church is related to believer's baptism?

Apply this same principle to social conditions. Should the practice of believer's baptism produce a community that is more safe,
just, and decent than other forms of Christian initiation? This question came to me often during my pastorate in Pittsburgh. That city
was largely Catholic and Presbyterian but had the lowest divorce
and crime rates of any major city in America, far less than some
baptist cities like Atlanta and Dallas.

If believer's baptism does not produce a higher degree of
Christian maturity or of social righteousness, what then? Shall we
abandon believer's baptism? No, but it will change the focus of our
defense of the practice. Modern scholarship consistently demonstrates that baptist-style baptism was the norm during New
Testament days. Thus, the baptist principle of restoration would
demand that we retain baptism; but the rationale would be weak-
ened. I think this is an issue that merits attention by church scholars.

Regardless of the relationship between baptism and disciple-ship, the church in America needs the insistence on faithfulness to God that arises (in part) out of the baptist vision. There is today too much that undermines this call to faithful living: the baptism of small children; the baptism of those whose testimony is weak and whose lives give no evidence of true conversion; the failure of the church (even baptist churches) to follow through with discipleship; the large number of "inactive church members" who avoid worship, ignore Scripture, fail to tithe, and never invest time or energy in the Lord's work. Such practices negate the baptist insistence upon faith-fulness to God. They also stand opposed to the apostolic insistence that Christians put away sin and put on Christ Jesus.

Believer's baptism is the public symbol of this baptist convic-tion of faithfulness to God. In a Sunday morning service at Third Baptist Church in Owensboro, we baptized three persons, two adults and one youth. The immersion part created problems. The people were adults, the water was high, my wading boots were too low. The water sloshed over the top of the boots and down on my clothes. That happened to me once before, while in Pittsburgh. On that occasion while the service continued I raced to the car, drove home, changed suits, and motored back to the church campus, and entered the worship service just as the minister of music said, "Let's sing one more stanza and hope the preacher will be here in time to preach the sermon!"

I remember another baptism, this one in Israel, at the Pool of Siloam. The water through Hezekiah's tunnel was low; thus the water in Siloam's Pool was low. In fact, it was barely knee-high. It is hazardous to baptize an adult in water that is too high. But it is exceedingly difficult to baptize by immersion an adult in water that is only knee-high. Perhaps that is why the Bible describes John the baptizer as locating "at Aenon near Salim, because there was plenty of water. . ." (John 3:23).

My point is this: in baptist-style Christianity, it is not the *mode* of baptism that is important, but rather the *meaning*. Indeed, there is good evidence that the first baptists (and even the first Baptists!) did not immerse, but rather practiced affusion (pouring). It is not how much water there is in the pool, but rather how much change there is in the person. It is the baptism of a believer, of a converted person, of a disciple, of a person committed to living a life faithful to God.

James I. Packer told a story at the Baptist Conference Center at Ridgecrest, North Carolina, in 1987. Packer, an Anglican (Episcopalian) and thus one who practiced infant sprinkling, recounted how the baptist preacher took the convert into the river. They reached the place where the water came to the knees. "Is this enough water?" the man asked the minister. "No" he replied and moved further, to where the water came to the waist. "This should be plenty of water," the convert said. But the baptist minister said not, and they moved even deeper into the river, to where the water rose above the chest. "Surely, there is sufficient water here to baptize me in a proper way," protested the candidate. "Yes, there is," said the minister. Whereupon he took the man and submerged him so that his head was fully covered by the water. Upon reemerging from the water, the newly baptized Christian said, "Just as I thought; it was the little bit of water on the head that was important."

The baby-boomer generation is bringing many changes to the way Christian people worship and organize. It is altogether proper for people to yearn for worship that is dynamic and energetic. It is necessary that people demand church-based programs for their children. It is understandable that people need for the church to address the very real concerns of daily living. But this consumer mentality does often reduce Christianity into one long version of this question, "What can the church do for me?"

The baptist insistence upon faithfulness to God and discipleship under the Lord Jesus Christ is an antidote that is very much needed in the American church. It takes the self-centered question of the immature believer and transforms it into the God-centered queries of the true disciple, "What can I do for the Lord? How must I change my ways? Where can I utilize my gifts and callings? Who needs the witness and the ministry that only I can give? When can I begin looking after the needs of others?" These are the true questions of Christian living. These are questions that are cultivated among baptist people. Their answers bring blessing to the whole world.

CHAPTER THREE

FREE IN THE WORD

THE BEREAN TYPE OF CHRISTIAN

Third Baptist Church of Owensboro, Kentucky has a Berean Sunday School class. Likewise, the landscape of Kentucky is dotted with Berean Baptist Churches. This name, so dear to baptists, comes from a story in the seventeenth chapter of Acts. It illustrates a principle that is at the heart of the baptist way of being Christians. Baptists are free in the Word of God.

The story relates how Paul and Silas entered Berea, a town in northern Greece. They went to the Jewish synagogue to teach about Jesus. This is how Luke describes the reaction of the Berean people: "Now the Bereans were of more noble character than the Thessalonians, for they received the message with great eagerness and examined the Scriptures every day to see if what Paul said was true" (Acts 17:11).

The Jewish synagogue was, and is, a gathering place for the study of scripture. The worship pattern of the first century synagogues included these features: reading of Hebrew Scriptures (Old Testament) in Hebrew; translation of Hebrew in the vernacular (Greek or Aramaic, etc); interpretation of the reading; discussion of the interpretation. According to one Jewish writer, the interpretation (or sermon) was to be given by "an elder (a member of the Sanhedrin), a sage, or by any distinguished person." Paul was easily a "distinguished person" if not a sage, having studied with Gamaliel in Jerusalem. Jewish synagogues throughout the Mediterranean world always welcomed these itinerant rabbis like Paul. This focus on the reading of Scripture and this openness to such visiting dignitaries provided just the environment needed for the implementation of Paul's missionary and church planting strategy.

When the people heard Paul teach, they examined the Scriptures every day to see if what he said was true. In other words, the lay people read the scriptures, discussed the matters, and debated the truth and wisdom of Paul's teaching. The people had both the freedom and the responsibility to hear with respect and evaluate with care what the apostle said. Later, John the apostle would encourage his readers to exercise discernment in such matters: "Dear friends, do not believe every spirit, but test the spirits to see whether they are from God, because many false prophets have gone out into the world." (1 John 4:1) It is this Berean spirit that has been a part of baptist life from the very beginning.

This freedom in the Word takes three forms. First, it is freedom to read the Bible. It is hard to believe that the Roman Catholic Church had put the Bible on the Index, that list of books which the laity were prohibited to read. It stayed on that Index until Vatican Council II (1963–1965). Since then there have been several first rate translations of the Bible for Catholic laity and there has been a groundswell of interest in the Bible throughout the Roman church.

From the very beginning of the baptist movement in the sixteenth century, priority has been given to each individual to own a Bible and to read a Bible. We are reminded of the words of the Apostle Paul to Timothy: "You know how from infancy you have known the holy Scriptures, which are able to make you wise for salvation through faith in Christ Jesus"(1 Tim. 3:15).

Third Baptist Church, Owensboro, gives Bibles to people, to infants at their dedication, to youth at graduation, to adults at their baptism, to deacons at their ordination. Baptist people are also active in such Bible distribution ministries as the Gideons and the various Bible societies.

I still have the Bible Third Baptist Church presented to me when I was installed as its pastor. I have in my hand tonight a little book that is about two inches square. It is the children's Bible given in 1944 to Nancy Russell, by the Nursery department of this church. Her father, a faithful member of our church, loaned it to me for this service tonight. This little book helped fulfill God's purpose in her life. Today, Nancy is an active leader in the Walnut Street Baptist Church of Louisville, Kentucky. Baptists believe that it is more important to have Bibles in the hands of the people than in the pews of the sanctuary.

Second, it is the freedom to interpret the Bible. Baptist people have avoided any appearance of telling people what they must believe and how they must interpret the Bible. "Read for yourself," we say. "Make up your own mind." Let every person search the scriptures and pray for the guidance of God's Spirit in discerning the meaning. This has been a hallmark of baptist life.

Walter Shurden, in his excellent book, *The Baptist Identity: Four Fragile Freedoms*, documents this tradition from the very earliest days of Southern Baptist life. In 1846, W. B. Johnson, the founder and first president of the Southern Baptist Convention, published a book on *Baptist Distinctives*. He listed five specific convictions that characterize baptists: (1) the sovereignty of God in salvation, (2) the supreme authority of the scripture, (3) the right of each individual to judge for himself in his views of truth as taught in the scriptures, (4) democratic church government, and (5) believer's baptism.

Dale Moody, the late Baptist theologian of world renown, often quoted a baptist document that recounted how baptists gathered for a service only to find themselves without a minister. These laypeople proceeded to open the Bible and read it, "each throwing his light as far as it would go." That is the baptist spirit.

A word should be said about Baptist confessions of faith. Baptists have never used such doctrinal statements to declare how an individual baptist must interpret the Bible; they are documents to show how some group of baptists have understood the Bible. The preamble to the 1925 "Baptist Faith and Message" states "that the sole authority for faith and practice among Baptists is the Scriptures of the Old and New Testaments. Confessions are only guides in interpretation, having no authority over the conscience."

Third, it is the freedom to teach the Bible. This applies to every person, including those who stand in the pulpit and those who stand behind classroom lecterns. It applies to the pastor of the church as well as the teacher in the classroom. Third Baptist Church has at least thirty-six Bible classes that meet every Sunday morning. There are thirty-five laypeople who prepare a lesson, who study the Bible, who gather their class, who teach the Word of God. There is one pastor who convenes the Pastor's Bible Class. All are free to teach the Bible as led by the Holy Spirit. This is not a license to teach heresy and promote immorality, but it is a liberty to share one's own interpretation of the Word of God.

This freedom to teach the Bible is at the heart of the current controversy among Southern Baptists. The fundamental issue is the proper balance between freedom and authority. Many feel threatened by this baptist tradition of freedom in reading the Bible. They think there has been too much freedom-style Christianity and that this freedom-style faith has brought Southern Baptists to the point of moral chaos, theological indifference, and spiritual lethargy. This description of Southern Baptist life has legitimized a call for new expressions of authority. "What is needed," they say, "are more authoritative creeds, more authoritative trustees, more authoritative pastors, more authoritative guidelines for confessing and living the Christian faith."

Such people wish to be baptist popes. One former president of the Southern Baptist Convention voiced his disgust at what some college and seminary teachers were saying in the classroom with these incredible words: "If we tell our teachers to teach that pickles have souls, then we expect them to teach that pickles have souls."

No, Mr. President, you are wrong! Your reckless speech betrays a fundamental misunderstanding of what it means to be a baptist-style Christian. You have actually invoked the substance and spirit of Catholic-style Christianity when you seek to control what baptists say and write. You have actually adopted the Protestant-style Christianity when you give doctrine greater priority than freedom in matters of the faith. Baptists are free in the Word of God. This freedom in the Word of God has shaped baptists as a people committed to reading and studying the Bible. It is at the center of our congregational worship and is the focal point of our personal spirituality.

I was called upon to preach the funeral message of Marjorie Clark. I did not know this long-time church member. I asked the family for her Bible, which they gladly handed to me. I could tell a great deal about Marjorie by inspecting her Bible. It was worn out, held together by tape. There is nothing more reassuring than a well-worn Bible. In this Bible were many printed items, clues to her spiritual life. There was a copy of the church covenant, a Bible-reading plan, a list of her Sunday School class members, a guide to important Bible verses, and a signed commitment card on which she confessed her faith in the saving power of the Lord Jesus Christ. The condition of her Bible and the materials contained therein were a powerful testimony to the freedom that she had to read the Bible, interpret the Bible and teach the Bible. It is a telling clue to what it means to be baptist.

May God bless every church with many more believers like Marjorie Clark. May God bring a blessing to the church of Jesus Christ through the baptist commitment to freedom in the Word.

CHAPTER FOUR

FAITHFUL TO THE WORD

DO WE NEED A NEW SHIBBOLETH?

J udges chapter twelve briefly records a rather obscure episode in the history of the Hebrew people. But that seemingly insignificant event has given western civilization a word and an idea that it has never forgotten. It is a word and an idea that bear directly upon what it means to be faithful to the Word of God.

There was bad blood between those Israelites who settled west of the Jordan River (Ephraim and Manasseh) and those who settled east, on the plateau of what is today known as Jordan (Gileadites). Judges describes one occasion when the Gileadites captured the fords of the Jordan. Some from Ephraim were trapped east of the Jordan. When they tried to conceal their identity in order to be allowed to cross at the fords, they were asked, 'Are you an Ephramite?' If they replied 'No' they were then asked to pronounce the word "Shibboleth." The dialect of the Ephraimites make their pronouncement of that word distinct; they said "Sibboleth." It is a difference between the "sh" and the "s" sound and it was enough to identify the enemy. Those who could not say "shibboleth" were killed.

Thus, a *shibboleth* is any word that signals that a person is part of a particular group. It is a verbal test of fellowship. Christian people of all kinds have used shibboleths to identify friends (the orthodox, the accepted, the safe) and to exclude enemies (the heretics, the excluded, the dangerous). The Nicean Creed insisted on the word *homoousion* (of one substance) rather than *homoiousion* (of like substance) when talking about Jesus' relation to the Father, (325 C.E.) A century later, *theotokos* (mother of God) was used to suppress heretics who were hesitant about the Marian doctrines.

Today there is a new shibboleth. It is the word *inerrancy*. It is the word that some are using to separate the true Christians from the false Christians, safe baptists from dangerous baptists. It is the word that many want to use to describe what it means to be faithful to the Word of God.

Baptists share with the Reformers of the sixteenth century a love for the Bible. Together we affirm that Holy Scripture is the supreme and sufficient authority for Christians. The confession of faith used by most Southern Baptists was originally penned as the "New Hampshire Confession of Faith" of 1833. It was slightly revised in 1853 by J. Newton Brown. In 1925, acting on behalf of the Southern Baptist Convention, E. Y. Mullins led a committee to revise and expand the confession. It was given the title "The Baptist Faith and Message." The first article reads:

> We believe that the Holy Bible was written by men divinely inspired, and is a perfect treasure of heavenly instruction; that it has God for its author, salvation for its end, and truth, without any mixture of error, for its matter; that it reveals the principles by which God will judge us; and therefore is, and shall remain to the end of the world, the true centre of Christian union, and the supreme standard by which all human conduct, creeds, and opinions should be tried.

What was intended to be "the true centre of Christian union" has become the chief source of Christian division in this century. In the last century, slavery was the issue that divided most of the religious groups, including Baptists (thus giving rise to the Southern Baptist Convention). But in these days, Scripture has driven a wedge between people and churches. Every major denomination in America has struggled with how to declare their faithfulness to the word of God.

The baptist way of faithfulness to the Word of God can be summarized as believing what it says, obeying what it commands, and hoping for what it promises.

The Bible tells a story that begins with creation and ends with the grand consummation of the ages in the return of our Lord Jesus and the defeat of the Evil One. The story includes chapters about Abraham and his travels, Moses and the Exodus, Joshua and the conquest of the Promised Land, David and the kingdom, Elijah and Elisha and the rise of prophecy, Shalmaneser and the fall of Israel, Nebuchadnezzar and the destruction of Jerusalem, Ezekiel and the Exile, and finally Ezra, Nehemiah and the rebuilding of Jerusalem.

In the New Testament, the story turns to the life, death and resurrection of Jesus followed by the development of the Christian churches throughout the Mediterranean world.

This story is told as a true story and we read it as a true story. It is not myth, fable, or invention. It is the history of God at work in the world. It is written for our edification; it is to inspire and instruct us. It is written for our participation; we become part of the story.

Baptist people believe what the Bible says. It speaks about sin and salvation, about righteousness and wickedness, about love and hate, and life and death. But the Bible does not say all that some people want it to say, and this is the point of contention. In telling the story, the Bible makes incidental references to ancient ways of life, economic features, social customs, cosmological ideas, historical assumptions, even geological patterns. Some people who are influential and articulate want to include these elements as part of the story we believe. They say that to believe the story is also to accept as important and inerrant all of these other matters. More than that, to believe the Bible is to transfer all of these ancient ways of thinking and assuming into the modern world. They charge that those who refuse to go along with this strategy deny the truth of God's word. This is the very doctrine that has gained ascendancy among the new leaders of the Southern Baptist Convention. This is the meaning of the word *inerrancy* as it is being used as a *shibboleth* among Christians today.

One of the best illustrations of this new method of interpretation is in regards to the opening chapters of Genesis. There, ancient cosmology is used to tell the story of how the eternal and omnipotent God spoke into existence the entire universe. The spiritual and theological message is about the difference between God and the created order, about the power of God, about the goodness of creation, about the uniqueness of the human race. But some interpreters want to make the geological and "scientific" elements of this story part of the divine truth that must be believed. This ideology is called scientific creationism. It is bad science and bad theology.

"Thy word is truth" says the prophet, and I say "Amen." But when modern would-be prophets take the lean meat of God's word and flavor it with salt and pepper and exotic spices and then bury it beneath gravy and serve it with assorted dishes to suit their own taste, I say, "No, thank you. A single piece of meat, broiled over an open fire, and served with a vegetable and a glass of water will be fine. It will provide all the nourishment I need. All the rest just clogs the arteries and expands the waistline."

We believe what the Bible says about what God has done for our redemption. Paul said that the scriptures are able to make us "wise unto salvation through faith in Christ Jesus" (2 Tim. 3:15). Thus we read the book as the plan of salvation and do not consult it as a manual for every other aspect of life and learning. We read it for moral guidance, but not necessarily for financial planning or military strategy.

Baptists try to obey what it commands, and the Bible has many commands. "Be fruitful, and multiply, and subdue the earth." "Honor your father and your mother." "Love your neighbor as yourself." "Give thanks to the Lord, for he is good." "Repent, and believe the good news, for the kingdom of God is at hand." "Do not judge." "Honor one another above yourself." The list is endless. Dale Moody was fond of quoting the great New Testament scholar J. A. Bengel (1687–1752): "Apply all of yourself to the Bible, and apply all of the Bible to yourself." Bengel was a Lutheran, but this is a baptist principle.

From the very beginning, this emphasis on obedience has characterized baptist life. Our intent was not so much to describe the Bible or debate its inspiration as it was to live according to its teaching. Donald F. Durnbaugh has highlighted this dimension of the baptist vision in his book *The Believers' Church: The History and Character of Radical Protestantism*. He quotes approvingly the Reformation baptist Hans Denck who said, "No one can truly know Jesus unless he follows Him in his life."

If there is one element that distinguished the baptist way of doing church it is this insistence upon actually living in conformity to the Word of God. This is the genius behind the idea of the regenerate church, believer's baptism, and church discipline. Members are received as they testify to a saving encounter with Jesus Christ, not because they can recite a specific doctrinal creed. Likewise, members are excluded for moral laxity, but rarely ever for theological deviation.

It is this wholehearted affirmation of the necessity of obedience that gave rise to the twin baptist efforts of ministry and missions. From the Mennonites of the sixteenth century to the Southern Baptists of the twentieth century, baptists have been known for their readiness to come to the aid of folks in need. Millions of meals were served in the wake of Hurricane Hugo in 1994. Eighty percent were donated and served by Southern Baptist ministry teams. Two hundred years before the larger, stronger churches of the Reformation took up the missionary endeavor, baptist people were taking seriously the command to go into all the world and preach the gospel. It was a baptist pastor, William Carey, who ignited the modern missions movement in the last decade of the eighteenth century, and the first non-Catholic missionary society in the West was organized and supported by baptists.

Baptists seek to obey what the Word commands: repent, believe, sacrifice, preach, serve, grow, learn, mature, and press on to the future that awaits us in Christ Jesus.

This brings us to the third and final element of a baptist understanding of faithfulness to the Word of God: we are called to hope for what it promises.

> Our citizenship is in heaven. And we eagerly await a Savior from
> there, the Lord Jesus Christ, who, by the power that enables him to
> bring everything under his control, will transform our lowly bodies
> so that they will be like his glorious body. Therefore, my brothers,
> that is how you should stand firm in the Lord. (Phil. 4:20–41)

A similar exposition of the resurrection of the body in 1
Corinthians chapter fifteen ends with an admonition to stand firm.

Baptist people have seen themselves as the eschatological
community. Sometimes this has been taken to excess with the resul-
tant and altogether misplaced confidence about the soon return of
Jesus. But better to err on that end of things than to become so lack-
adaisical about the coming Kingdom that we lose touch with the
purifying power of the blessed hope. John the Apostle wrote,
"Everyone who has this hope in him purifies himself" (1 John 3:3).

Baptists hold dear to the Word of God, even if many cannot in
good conscience pronounce the shibboleth that has become the
word of division and death for many modern-day Ephraimites. The
biblical story of the shibboleth is set on a battlefield. It is no accident
that some baptists today see their calling as a crusade against those
who refuse to pronounce the sacred word *inerrancy*. Harold Lindsell,
the late baptist writer and theologian, published a book in 1976 that
has set the tone on baptist relations for the two decades. It was
entitled *Battle for the Bible*. With this image of warfare, he advocated
the use of *inerrancy* as a shibboleth, as a means of determining who
are friends and who are foes to the gospel of the Lord Jesus Christ.

To be fair, the clamor for inerrancy may be fueled by a genuine
desire to defend the Bible from those who would strip it of its
authority and power, or those who through radical biblical criti-
cism would strip it of its divine inspiration and trustworthiness.
But such people do not live among baptists. People such as
baptists are not among those who need to speak some sacred shibboleth to declare their loyalty to Jesus, his Word, and his way. We
believe in our hearts and declare with our lips that his Word is
true. We declare with our lives that his way leads to life and happi-
ness. We declare with our hearts that his promises are certain. This
is enough.

CHAPTER FIVE

FREE IN THE CHURCH

THE FIRST GREAT BAPTIST LEADER

Free and faithful baptists found their first great leader in
Balthasar Hubmaier of Zurich (although Baptists with a
capital *B* would not appear until the early 1600s). A priest
and a professor of the Roman Catholic Church, Hubmaier was
assigned to the parish at Waldshut where he came under the influence of the famous Reformation leader Ulrich Zwingli.

Reformation, however, was not enough: Hubmaier was soon
convicted that what was needed was nothing short of the restoration of the New Testament church. Hubmaier embraced the efforts
of the radical reformers, the Anabaptists. "The great Christian
revolutions," wrote H. Richard Niebuhr, "come not by discovery
of something that was not known before. They happen when
somebody takes radically something that was always there."

So it was with baptists and so it was with Hubmaier. He
believed only converted adults should be received for baptism;
and those who entered the Christian church must renounce the
world and live a life consecrated to God. Hubmaier published
these doctrines of the free and faithful congregation in one of the
first volumes of baptist theology, *On the Indestructibility of Truth.*

The rulers of both church and state were frightened by
Hubmaier and his radical ideas of freedom and faithfulness. He
was captured, tortured and forced to recant. Upon escape he
renounced his recantation and took up the pen again in the cause

of biblical restorationism. In 1528, Hubmaier was again detained, extradited to Vienna, tied to a stake in a public square, and set afire. Balthasar Hubmaier thus became the first great martyr in the cause of free and faithful baptists.

The followers of Hubmaier were called Swiss Brethren. Like-minded people in others places in Europe were called Anabaptists, Hutterites and Mennonites. In England they were known as Nonconformists and Dissenters. They were the ancestors of this great tradition in which we now stand: baptist people, free and faithful baptist people. They believed that faith and holiness could not be coerced; that people were free to confess Christ or reject Christ; that only believers should be received into the church; that church members covenanted together to live a life pleasing to the Lord; that congregations were free to gather for worship, write their doctrine, call their pastor, and direct their affairs, all without the interference of either secular or sacred authorities; and that only the Holy Scripture held supreme authority for Christian people.

The baptist movement was birthed in the struggle for freedom over against the authority of pope and prince, king and cardinal, council and congress.

Free and faithful baptists have always led the struggle for freedom against the forces of control, conformity, and creedalism. We find our scriptural mandate set forth clearly in that most powerful of all biblical writings, Paul's letter to the Galatians:

> It is for freedom that Christ has set us free. Stand firm, then, and do not let yourselves be burdened again by a yoke of slavery. . . . But do not use your freedom to indulge the sinful nature; rather, serve one another in love (5:1, 13).

Our Lord Jesus himself is the best example of an individual who embodied these fundamental principles of freedom and faithfulness. It is Christ whom we follow as baptist Christians. Following Christ has led baptists to advocate what has come to be called the free church.

A free church is a congregation of believers, all of whom are encouraged to exercise their spiritual gifts in the power of the Holy Spirit. This is at the heart of what baptists mean by "the priesthood of every believer." A pivotal text for baptist people has been Acts 2 with its inclusive statement about the Spirit: "I will pour out my Spirit on all people"(Acts 2:17; cf. Joel 2:28). It is interesting that several groups of baptist Christians—specifically laypeople, women, missionaries, and Pentecostals—find in this text a foundational statement of Christian existence. Formal distinctions are blurred as all find their ministry among God's people.

A free church is a congregation of believers, each individually empowered to participate in the decisions of the group. This "communal discernment," as baptist theologian James W. McClendon Jr. calls it, consists of a deliberate seeking of God's will in such matters as doctrinal statements, scriptural interpretations, officer selection and ordination, organizational life, property decisions, and church discipline. Baptists pioneered the democratic idea of church life. All are equal and each is responsible.

A free church is a congregation that gladly and voluntarily enters into fraternal association with other like-minded baptist people. Cooperation cannot be coerced and controlled by those inside or outside the congregation. Churches are free before God and within the Christian community. Thus, baptist people have been eager to unite in associations for fellowship and support and in conventions for missionary and benevolent purposes.

For twenty years baptist people in America have carried on a great debate over what it means to be a baptist-style Christian. The defining issue has been the choice between freedom and authority. Those who champion the need for authority contend that the issue is truth versus error. This has always been the contention of those who wield power in the name of God. This was exactly the rationale of those who lit the match that sent Balthasar Hubmaier home to glory. "We must defend the truth against the infidels," they cry. Such rhetoric is the emotional fuel of crusades.

In 1979, the "defenders of truth" launched a crusade to "save" the institutions and agencies of the Southern Baptist Convention from theological apostasy and moral bankruptcy. It seems that there was too much freedom, and the time was right for the exercise of authority. James T. Draper, then president of the Southern Baptist Convention, published a book entitled *Authority: The Critical Issue for Southern Baptists* (Revell, 1984).

A history of the resolutions introduced and approved by these who claim to continue the tradition of baptists gives us insight into their character. In 1984, women were denied their freedom and relegated to subservient status in the church. Then in 1988, laypeople were put in their place, as the pastor was elevated as the ruler of the people. That same 1988 resolution, in an appalling piece of historical revisionism, reduced the baptist ideal of the priesthood of every believer to secondary status and discounted it as of recent vintage.

Some of you know what it is like to live under the control of authority-minded leaders. For several months Third Baptist Church had, in its evening worship services, a large contingent of baptist people from a neighboring county. They were members of what was once one of the largest and strongest Baptist churches in the area. But a new spirit entered their pulpit and people, a spirit that treasured not freedom but authority. To find a time and place to be free and faithful baptists, these people had to leave the established church and seek a better place. For several months they have had congregational worship on Sunday morning. Attendance the first Sunday was almost seventy people. God bless these free and faithful baptists.

One more story will serve to illustrate how this struggle between freedom and authority has emerged as the focal point of debate about the baptist way of being Christian. A few years ago a local paper carried the news of the election of Jim Henry as president of the Southern Baptist Convention. I was quoted as saying it was "the first good news we have had in fifteen years." Henry was the independent candidate running against the man handpicked by the small college of "baptist cardinals" that had managed our Southern Baptist Convention for more than a decade. Henry's election was a surprise. It was a victory for those who were tired of the controlling tactics of our new leaders. One of the neo-baptist leaders, recently installed as pastor of the largest church in the Southern Baptist Convention, tried to explain Henry's victory with these words: "For fifteen years we needed the assault troops. But now, Henry is leading the occupation forces."

Occupation forces? What is the meaning of this language? Why use this terminology of war and violence? In 1979, Judge Paul

Pressler of Houston launched this crusade with another violent image: "We are going for the jugular." It is unbelievable that a baptist minister would describe his relation with other baptist people in terms of an army of occupation or (to use Judge Pressler's rhetoric) a knife to the throat. It is ungodly, it is unacceptable, and it is against the words and spirit of Jesus our Lord. It is especially out of place among baptists because of our emphasis on the voluntary element in true religion—faith and participation must be uncoerced.

I prefer the words of W. A. Criswell when, early in his ministry at the First Baptist Church of Dallas, he wrote a testimony for the book edited by Joe Odle entitled *Why I Am a Baptist* (Broadman, 1972). Criswell wrote:

> I find myself in an ecclesiastical atmosphere that is not only true to the New Testament but one that also blesses my own heart and spirit. I am free in my work in my pulpit ministry, in the explanation of my convictions. I am completely, absolutely, everlastingly free. There is no bishop, there is no hierarchy, there is no machine, there is no overlording ecclesiastical authority to tell me when, where, what, how, and anything else. I can be myself, truly and really, being a Baptist. I love this. I am dedicated to this. I would have it no other way.

I have this to say to those who threaten to intimidate free and faithful baptists with such shocking language. When you see soldiers in this army of occupation, tell them that your pastor is a free and faithful baptist. When you see these agents of enforced conformity, tell them you are a member of a free church, an outpost of liberty, and a center of the resistance to this army of occupation. When some general in this occupation force seeks to control your mind, your money, your faith, and your freedom, look them in the eye as a free and faithful baptist and say, in the words of Holy Scripture, "It is for freedom that Christ has set me free. I will not submit again to a yoke of slavery"(Gal. 5:1).

CHAPTER SIX

FAITHFUL TO THE CHURCH

SAM JONES COMES TO TOWN

S am Jones, Methodist evangelist from Cartersville, Georgia, came to Owensboro in 1893 and 1895. His conversational yet confrontational style of preaching did its work on Baptist pastor Fred Hale. Hale had come to the pastorate of Owensboro's First Baptist Church in February of 1893. Under the influence of Jones's vision and rhetoric, Hale led his church in such a way as to precipitate a division. In August of 1896, Hale led the majority of members as they walked out of the sanctuary, while those who remained behind stood and sang, "God Be With You 'Till We Meet Again." The new congregation was called Third Baptist Church.

In his first sermon in May of 1893, Sam Jones said: "Anybody can be a Methodist in Owensboro on a mighty low plane. Now you Presbyterians, Baptists and Christians sit there and grin. I mean all of you. You are no better than the Methodists about that. You can be a good church member in Owensboro and not amount to much."

Jones's message fell on receptive ears among Christian people of Daviess County and the surrounding areas. They recognized his words as a call for the restoration of the tradition of disciplined Christian living and a covenanted church life. The particular practice then in question was alcohol; but the more

36

fundamental issue was the matter of church discipline. Does a Christian church expect its members to adhere to certain moral and ethical standards as a condition of church membership and, more fundamentally, as a condition of Christian discipleship? The preaching of an evangelist like Sam Jones is as much needed today as it was one hundred years ago.

The baptist movement, from its origin in the sixteenth century, has put a high priority on Christian discipleship as a way of life. It was the reformation of life rather than the reformation of doctrine that set the baptists apart from the sixteenth century protestant reformers of the church. Thus, the church covenant (the guide to Christian living) was as prominent as the confession of faith (the guide to Christian thinking).

It may well be that the church covenant as a guide to Christian living has played a role among baptists that is unique in the Christian movement. It indeed constitutes one of the more valuable contributions of baptists to a complete understanding of what it means to be the church of Jesus Christ in our world.

The chief expression of the disciplined Christian life was the gathered church. The gathered church was composed of those who actually attended the meetings of the church and who sought to live according to the church covenant.

In opposition to the gathered church was the territorial church, which was the hallmark of both Catholic and Protestant churches. Territorial churches included all people who lived within a certain geographical boundary, regardless of their involvement in the spiritual life of the congregation. In 1648, after years of religious conflict, the civil and ecclesiastical leaders of Europe concluded the Peace of Westphalia in which they affirmed the principle of *cuius regio, eius religio,* a Latin phrase which means "as the prince, so the religion." The symbol of this inclusiveness was infant baptism, in which initiation of a person into Christian community was not connected with their profession of faith or express intent to live in obedience to Christ.

In stark contrast to infant baptism and the territorial church, the mark of the gathered church was believer's baptism. Only adults who freely and publicly professed their faith and committed themselves to walk in the way of Christ were initiated into the church. These baptized converts agreed to live in accordance with the covenant of the church.

Third Baptist Church is a covenanted congregation. In 1896, its founding members adopted the "New Hampshire Church Covenant." This covenant had been written in 1833, but was later revised by J. Newton Brown and published in *The Baptist Church Manual* in 1853. The founders of Third adopted the original 1833 version of this covenant. They also adopted "Special Rules, Made Because of the Exigencies of the Times in Owensboro." These extra rules forbade any contact with alcoholic beverages, dancing, and card playing. All three had been vigorously denounced by Sam Jones. Rule four excluded church members who failed to attend or contribute during the course of a calendar year.

In 1904, the covenant of Third Baptist Church was revised to conform to the 1853 New Hampshire Church Covenant. This 1853 version included a ban on alcohol, and Third Church added a phrase to prohibit dancing and cards. This revised covenant was re-approved in 1976. The covenant currently printed in the church constitution has deleted the references to dancing and cards.

Every church needs to write or adopt a church covenant. There is something noble about a church that takes a stand on specific matters of Christian morality. It is true that today there is little sympathy for a group of people proscribing how an individual should live. But the church covenant is a document to which people freely subscribe. Coercion in matters of conduct is as foreign to the baptist vision as coercion in matters of doctrine.

As regards the covenant tradition of Third Church, I say without apology that I appreciate the ban on alcohol; but I would support an extension to include all recreational drugs, including tobacco. Our culture is awash in a sea of drugs, and baptist churches, like baptist homes, need to provide an island of self-control for people who want to escape the danger and disease associated with drugs. We need places, parties, and personal networks free of the social use of drugs.

I could live with the prohibition on dancing, as it protects me from what could be rather embarrassing dance floor displays. But I like my cards. At least once a day, I lay out my face cards for a game of solitaire. And I remember one of the first social events I attended in Owensboro was an after-church card game at the home of Alvey and Helen Smith. They were using, however, Baptist cards, otherwise known as Rook!

While the covenant is intended to be a positive, pro-active document designed to clarify expectations and encourage righteous living, it has too often been used in a negative way. Very early in the history of church covenants, there developed the ban, that action on the part of local congregations to discipline individuals whose behavior did not conform to the covenant guidelines. Article seventeen of the Short Confession of Faith in XX Articles by John Smyth reads: "That brethren who persevere in sins known to themselves, after the third admonition, are to be excluded from the fellowship of the saints by excommunication."

In 1527 the Swiss Brethren issued the Schleitheim Confession. It consists of seven articles dealing with: baptism, excommunication, communion, separation, pastors, swords and oaths.

> We agree as follows on the ban: The Ban shall be employed with all those who have given themselves to the Lord, to walk in His commandments, and with all those who have been baptized into the one body of Christ and who are called brethren and sisters, and yet who slip sometimes and fall into error and sin, being inadvertently overtaken. The same shall be admonished twice in secret and the third time openly disciplined or banned according to the command of Christ. (Matt. 18) But this shall be done according to the regulation of the Spirit (Matt. 5) before the breaking of bread, so that we may break and eat one bread, with one mind and in one love, and may drink of one cup (Article two).

Too often the word *discipline* has been used as a synonym for *punishment* or *dismissal* or *excommunication.* Typical is the book

Church Discipline by J. D. Maddor published in 1911. It is a populist appeal to the ideal of an ordered and disciplined congregation. The opening lines read:

> Three failures on the part of many of our churches really menace them. First in importance, is the failure to guard carefully the door of entrance, so that many gain entrance to membership in our churches who give no evidence of regeneration. Second in importance, is the failure to properly indoctrinate the churches. . . . Third, and of very great and grave importance, is the failure to exercise wise and wholesome corrective discipline over their members; so that we tolerate in our members that which we ought not to tolerate, and retain as members men and women who would be better 'put from among' us.

The spirit and substance of this heavy emphasis on the negative side of church discipline is summed up in his quote from a booklet entitled "The Barren Fig Tree," by J. B. Moody in which one who lives "in unholy wedlock, or rents his property for evil purposes, or . . . uses bad language, etc., and defies the church" is to be banned. Moody urges: "Get your pick and dig him out root and branch."

The records of Third Baptist Church of Owensboro, Kentucky, illustrate further how the covenant was frequently used in a negative way, that is, to exclude someone from membership for behavior which violated the covenant. The minutes of the meeting of the Board of Deacons read:

> April 28, 1898: "Moses Thorpe having reported in case of Brother ——— who had been guilty of drunkenness and that he had promised to lead a better life. Brother Thorpe was instructed to cite him to appear before the church at the next church business meeting at which time charges would be preferred against him." [Records show the member cited was excluded from the church membership in August 1898.]

> July 5, 1898: "Brother Moses Thorpe reported that ——— denied the charge of swearing. Report was received and committee of Moses Thorpe discharged."

September 2, 1897: "It being reported that ———— had been guilty of playing cards and dancing, Deacon G. W. Mullen was appointed to see him."

September 30, 1897: "James H. Parrish continued as a committee to see ————, there have been additional rumors as to bad character."

Such official church action has given covenants (and churches!) a bad name. Their use primarily in a negative fashion illustrates what Philip Yancy has called "ungrace." Many churches preach grace and practice ungrace. The ban distorts both the essence of the gospel and the ideal of discipleship.

This ungraceful use of covenants has led to their gradual disuse in modern church life. This is regrettable. It is time for a renaissance of covenanted churches. In a time of moral confusion both in the church and in society, a church covenant can function as a powerful and effective means of cultivating mature and effective disciples of Jesus Christ.

There is a positive way to use the church covenant. To begin with, we recognize that covenants are biblical. God made a covenant with Noah (Gen. 9), with Abraham (Gen. 12, 13, 15, 17, and 22), with the Hebrew people through Moses (Exod. 20–30), and with David and his descendants (2 Sam. 7).

Jeremiah foresaw a day when God would make a new covenant with Israel in which He would write His word on the heart of every one and put His spirit on every one (Jer. 31:31–34). Jesus transformed the Jewish Passover supper into Christian Communion, with these words, "This cup . . . is the new covenant in my blood" (Luke 22:20).

The book from which we read the word of God is a covenant book. It includes the old covenant, a history of God's dealings with Israel. It includes the new covenant, a description of the life and teaching of Jesus. Our word *testament* is but a translation of the word *covenant*. The Bible is a covenant book.

Baptist people are covenant people. We believe that church life is to be regulated by some form of common agreement as to what behavior is consistent with Christian beliefs. After preaching on the subject "Free in the Church" and advocating the baptist vision of radical freedom, one person in our congregation challenged me with this statement: "It will lead to anarchy."

It is true that freedom without some means to establish accountability, responsibility, or faithfulness leads to moral and doctrinal chaos. But baptists have a way of mutual accountability—it is the church covenant. The covenant, which baptist people often read during worship services, commits each of us to mutual care, moral discernment, spiritual discipline, and congregational order. The church covenant is a practical means to avoid anarchy and establish moral order.

A new challenge to baptist life today comes from a new category of church membership. Whereas the "gathered church" principle powerfully challenged the "territorial churches" of Medieval and Reformation Europe, the challenge today comes from the "enrolled church." Third Church, through one hundred years of history, has become an "enrolled church." There are more than 1900 enrolled as members of this church. Less than half are functioning members of the congregation and more than 700 are nonresident! This creates the inactive church member. Inactive church members and nonresident church members constitute (with some exceptions), according to baptist understanding of the church, a contradiction in terms.

One way to promote covenant responsibility and maintain our historic commitment to disciplined living is through an annual covenant signing. The church covenant could be displayed in the church building throughout the year. Each year each member would be requested to sign the covenant. This signing would then constitute a recommitment of the person to a life of faithfulness to Jesus Christ and his church. At the end of the year all members who had signed the covenant during the year (and only those people) would be continued as members of the church. Special arrangements could be made for homebound and certain nonresident persons (for instance, college students, military personnel, etc.). This process is consistent with the baptist principle of uncoerced religion; it freely allows people to maintain a covenant relationship with the church as they feel called by Christ.

Scholars of religion who survey the contemporary scene tell us of declining loyalty to church life. It has become a consumers' market with Christian people shopping around for the most attractive church program, the most exciting worship style, and the most compatible biblical interpretation. Against this trend of freedom without faithfulness, baptist churches have the opportunity to practice a Christian discipleship that guards the freedom of both the person and the congregation. Yet it holds both the person and the congregation in a covenanted relationship that cultivates the gifts and graces of Jesus Christ.

CHAPTER SEVEN

FREE IN THE WORLD

AMOS WAS A BAPTIST PREACHER

A mos was the eighth century prophet from Tekoah, a village located in the hill country of Judah. God called him from tending sheep and fruit trees to preach His word in Bethel, a center of Israelite religious life situated in the northern country of Israel. Amos declared the judgment of God upon Israel for their wicked living and distorted religion.

The message of Amos was not well received. The priest at Bethel, Amaziah, reported to King Jereboam the words of Amos. Amaziah confronted Amos, perhaps on the orders of Jereboam, and said: "Get out, you prophet! Go back to the land of Judah. Earn your bread there and do your prophesying there. Don't preach anymore at Bethel, because this is the king's sanctuary and the temple of the kingdom" (Amos 7:10–17). The king had heard enough of the prophet's message, and he ordered his pastor to expel this itinerant preacher from the territory.

This was neither the first nor the last time that some civil authority has attempted to control the free exercise of religion. It is just one more illustration of how and why religion needs to be free in this world.

The marriage of religion and government was a standard feature of life in Israel. This is reflected throughout the Old Testament. King David, the epitome of leadership, was called the "anointed one of God." He was both spiritual and civil leader of

Israel. Religion gave legitimacy to political power; and political power authorized religious values.

Priests and princes have always been tempted by this marriage of convenience. This has been true even within the Christian tradition. Constantine became emperor of the Roman empire in the year 312 of the Christian era. Later, he converted to Christianity and made it the official religion of the empire. By the time of his death, he had assumed the role of leader of both church and state and had bound them in a powerful partnership that persisted through the Middle Ages.

The Reformers of the sixteenth century challenged much of Roman Catholic religion, but the marriage of church and state was not one of them. The Reformers made their own alliances with the regional princes of Europe. The growing nationalism of Europe, united with religious fervor, paved the way for one hundred years of religious wars.

While Catholics and Protestants contended for political power, another group quietly advocated the radical separation of church and state. These were the baptist people of Europe and England. They were Swiss Brethren, Anabaptists, Hutterites, Mennonites, Dissenters, Nonconformists, and Puritans. These baptist people believed that the best way to ensure authentic Christianity was to free the church from the state and free the state from the church.

This was the pattern they found in the New Testament. The early Christians had no political power or civil alliances. They were marginalized and powerless people, gathering in homes, in synagogues, at riverbanks, and in marketplaces. They confessed Christ as Lord, shared goods with those in need, practiced self-control, and advocated equality among all peoples in the sight of God. When they came into conflict with civil authorities, they asked the question: "Judge for yourselves whether it is right in God's sight to obey you rather than God" (Acts 4:19). The baptist movement of the sixteenth and seventeenth centuries attempted to restore this New Testament pattern, including the freedom of religious expression.

Roger Williams was one of the most famous advocates of this radical idea of religious freedom. He was a Puritan preacher who immigrated to the New World in order to find freedom in spiritual things. But he discovered that the religious leaders of the

Massachusetts Bay Colony, while rejecting the established Church of England, also rejected all who deviated from their version of Christian living. Williams fled to the wilderness, bought land from the Narragansett Indians, and settled the first colony known for religious toleration: Rhode Island. There, Roger Williams wrote his famous books advocating what he called "soul-liberty," the freedom of each settler to worship only as his or her conscience dictated. It was the first radical experiment in the separation of church and state.

Baptist people influenced the architects of the American republic in their ideas of religious freedom. Virginia baptist preacher John Leland personally lobbied James Madison who, in turn, drafted the first amendment to the Constitution of the United States. It reads: "Congress shall make no law respecting an establishment of religion or prohibiting the free exercise thereof." This is the first freedom of the American people.

From time to time, baptist people are tempted to forsake their tradition of freedom and enter into alliances with secular power. Sometimes it appears to be in the best interest of both church and state. The church may want to assist the state in teaching and supporting moral and ethical values; or the state may desire the stamp of approval that the church can give.

In our day there is enormous pressure for baptist churches to accept an engagement ring from the political authorities. Nowhere is this more crucial than in the arena of public education. Many religious leaders, on the one hand, wish to influence what is taught and said (and prayed!) in public schools. These same religious leaders, on the other hand, want the government to support religious schools with tax money. Political leaders see this strategy both as a way to please a voting electorate and as a way to address the very real issues of disorder and immorality in our country. While there is growing and legitimate concern about the need for religious values and voices to be heard in matters of public policy, the entanglement of church and state is a danger that baptist people have long protested.

Throughout the world, there has never been greater need for this baptist witness. Israel, Iran, and the old Soviet republics illustrate the damage to gospel witness when the state makes an alliance with a particular religious group. In Israel, it is the Jewish faith; in Iran, it is Islam; in the Soviet republics, it is the Russian Orthodox church. In all these places, baptist people are being persecuted, and in some instances even martyred. In all of these places, the cry is for freedom: religious freedom, spiritual freedom, church freedom, and soul freedom. The baptist conviction is this: God's kingdom thrives best when local churches are free of control and intimidation, free to live out the gospel, free to preach the gospel, and free to call Jesus Lord.

The best, most powerful contribution that baptist people can make to the peace and welfare of a nation is by establishing and maintaining congregations of people living in covenant agreement with one another and with the Lord Jesus Christ. These congregations thus provide, visible to the public, an alternative to the often immoral, irresponsible lifestyles that may characterize a given community. This is, in essence, a counter-culture approach to the relationship between church and community and between church and government. This strategy protects the freedom of both the congregation and the civil authorities. This is the baptist way of being a Christian church.

Amos was a baptist preacher. He was free before God, free to receive His message and free to declare His message. Amaziah was pastor of the congregation in Bethel, but he seems to have sold his soul to King Jereboam. Likewise, the congregation at Bethel appears to have lost its freedom to hear and respond to the word of God because of their desire to please the king. But thank God the king could not squelch the preaching of Amos. While there was no baptist congregation, in Amos there was a baptist preacher.

I am reminded of another baptist preacher, John Bunyan. In seventeenth century England, his baptist way of following Christ aroused the ire of the ruling party. He spent twelve years in the local jail in Bedford. While there he preached the good news of Jesus Christ, and he wrote one of the most famous pieces of English literature, *The Pilgrim's Progress*.

Thank God for the examples as Amos the baptist prophet, John Bunyan the baptist preacher, and Roger Williams the baptist pioneer. They stir up within us the determination to treasure our baptist heritage of freedom. In this world, and in all places, let the church be free.

CHAPTER EIGHT

FAITHFUL TO THE WORLD

ATTEMPT GREAT THINGS FOR GOD

O n Main Street in Lexington, Kentucky, there stands in front of the County Clerk's office an historical marker. The plaque marks the spot of the Main Street Christian Church, established in 1842, and the text recounts the sixteen-day debate in 1843 between Alexander Campbell and Nathan Rice. The moderator was the honorable senator from Kentucky, Henry Clay. This debate was one of the more famous episodes in that double decade of turbulence among Christian people in what was then the West, as they sought to discern the truth about the New Testament and about the way baptist people read and interpret the Scriptures.

Campbell came to America from Scotland with his father, Thomas. They settled in western Pennsylvania and affiliated with one of the churches of the old Redstone Baptist Association. The Campbell vision was of a unified Christian movement, centered on Christian love and the Bible. The movement they launched was known then and now as the Restoration movement. However, instead of uniting the already diverse Christian churches into one, the Campbells succeeded only in further splintering the Christian movement. Their followers, known for years informally as Campbellites, are now known by such names as Church of Christ, Christian Church, and Disciples of Christ.

The historical significance of the Campbellite controversy was the debate it aroused as to the essential characteristics of the baptist movement. One chief issue was missions. The first baptist missionary convention had been held in 1814 (The Triennial Convention), and promoters like John Mason Peck and Luther Rice traveled across the frontier (which included Kentucky) to promote the cause of home and world missions.

The baptist missionaries ran into opposition from Campbell and his followers, especially John Taylor and Daniel Parker. These men led what became known as the "anti-mission movement." They contended that neither the New Testament nor baptist tradition gave support to this vision of world evangelization.

Quite the opposite is the truth. I find in baptist theology and practice three elements that challenge baptists of all generations to take seriously the responsibility to be faithful to the world in the preaching of the Gospel.

First, baptist people read the New Testament as if it is speaking directly to us. Acts chapter sixteen records Paul's vision of the Macedonia call. We travel with Paul through Asia; we feel his frustration when his plans to go north are blocked; we are with him in Troas when he meets the unnamed person; and (I say this with caution) we are in his bedroom when the vision comes. His call is our call. His reaction is our reaction. Paul and his companions "got ready at once to leave for Macedonia, concluding that God had called us to preach the gospel to them" (Acts 16:10).

Because there is embedded in the New Testament a missionary vision, there is embedded in the mind and heart of every true baptist a similar missionary vision. Jesus spoke to us when he said: "Go, make disciples of every nation, baptizing them . . . and teaching them . . . and I will be with you" (Matt. 28:19–20).

Norm and Martha Lytle were baptist missionaries in Israel when my wife, Jan, and I lived there in 1973 and 1974. They befriended us in every way and often hosted us in their beautiful home on the Mount of Olives overlooking the old city of

Jerusalem. Later Norm and Martha went to Russia. They served as coordinators of Southern Baptist mission work in the republics of the old Soviet Union. It is a modern-day Macedonia. Christians all over the west see a vision of a Russian person saying, "Come over into Russia and help us."

Second, we practice the priesthood of all Christians. This universal priesthood commissions each of us to speak to God on behalf of people (through prayer) and to speak to people on behalf of God (as evangelists). In other words, when our priest-hood is reduced to the privilege of direct communication with God or the freedom to read the Bible for ourselves, it is a half calling. The full calling involves the ministry of the good news of Jesus Christ.

First Peter 2:9 reads likes this: "You are a chosen people, a royal priesthood, a holy nation, a people belonging to God that you may declare the praises of him who called you out of dark-ness into his wonderful light." Peter is actually quoting a passage from the Old Testament, Exodus 19:6. This very clearly says that a chief purpose of our priesthood is the privilege to declare for all to hear what God has done for us in Christ.

It is this missionary priesthood that blurs the distinction between clergy and laity. It is not so much that we de-emphasize the ordination of a pastor as it is that we emphasize the ordina-tion of the people. Your baptism is your ordination to Christian ministry. All of us, a royal priesthood, are called upon to share the good news of Jesus Christ.

It was some women whom John Bunyan overheard as they gossiped the gospel in a doorway in Bedford, England. He was converted from outright wickedness through religious reform to genuine Christ-centered repentance, as he later described in his book *Grace Abounding to the Chief of Sinners*. Bunyan became an influential baptist leader and a world-renowned writer. His life and ministry were the result of people, pew people, taking seri-ously their priesthood. This is the foundation of baptist faithfulness to the people of world.

There is a third reason, and the conversion of John Bunyan illustrates it in a wonderful way. Baptist people are those people who, first of all, can testify to an evangelical experience of grace, or conversion. From the very beginning, our meetings have often been simply testimonials, in which one by one people stand to testify to their experience of the risen Lord. People who can testify are believers and are therefore candidates for believer's baptism.

Because we have had this experience with Christ, we are sure others can and will. Therefore, we invite people to hear the gospel, believe the gospel, and live the gospel. The evangelical invitation is thus a constituent part of what it means to be baptist. We hold dear not so much the baptism of believers (even though that has given us a name and a public image) but rather the conversion event and experience of believers.

One day years ago while visiting the parents of my wife, I picked up the conversion testimony of Charles Colson. It is a book entitled *Born Again*. It held me spellbound; and I was not surprised to discover later that Colson had been baptized and had affiliated with a baptist church. His personal experience of transforming grace is right at the center of what it means to be baptist.

True baptists are therefore missionary and evangelistic people. Not all baptists have agreed with this. On another occasion, while a guest in the home of my wife's parents, I once again picked up a book to read. It was the history of Cade's Cove. The early settlers of that beautiful valley in eastern Tennessee included my wife's ancestors. The settlers formed a baptist church. But the debate over missions crept into the cove and into the church. The baptist people divided, so the book recounts; and there emerged out of this debate a missionary baptist church and a primitive baptist church. While the primitive baptists, those who repudiated mission activity, held onto the baptist name, they discarded the true baptist vision.

True baptists understand and echo the convictions of the Apostle Paul when he wrote: "I am obligated both to Greeks and non-Greeks, both to the wise and the foolish. That is why I am so eager to preach the gospel also to you who are at Rome" (Romans 1:14–15). Thus Paul was both free in the world and faithful to the world. Like baptists today he was free of constraint, control, and intimidation by either ecclesiastical or civil authorities. But he was faithful to the people of the world, faithful to his missionary and evangelistic calling "to declare the praises of him who called us out of darkness into his marvelous light" (1 Peter 2:10).

Throughout this twentieth century, baptists have played a prominent role in the vitality of the Christian mission. Through wars and rumors of war, through poverty, pain, and persecution unparalled in world history, through tyranny, torture, and times of great distress, baptists have been strengthened by their heritage of liberty in Christ; they have remained centered in their faithfulness to the mission of Christ.

Who knows the coming century? Who knows what opportunities, what oppressions? Who knows what revolutions, what persecutions? Who knows the rise and fall of nations, the up and down of fortunes, the ebb and flow of life itself? Who knows but God only!

Christian living in the twenty-first century, as in the two millennia gone before, will find its sustaining power in the beautiful, bountiful presence of the Risen Lord. Baptist Christians, then as before, will bear witness to Christ and thus serve to sustain the global mission of Christ by clinging to those twin gifts bestowed upon us. Let us treasure as from God above the gift of freedom; let us treasure as from the Lord of Heaven the gift of faithfulness; and in this way work and witness yet another century in the fullness of the Spirit of life.